The Jay Way is an uncommon Take

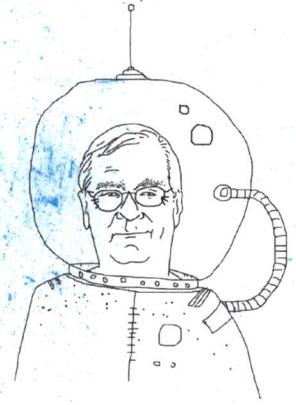
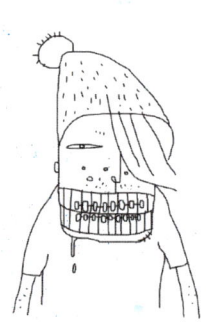

IT'S SENIORS AND JUNIORS

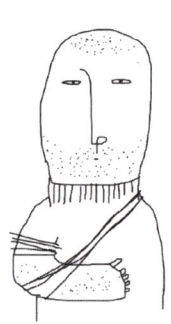

AND NEVER BEFORE'S

you're MUCH better looking, and MUCH MUCH smarter too

It doesn't take luggage but pack some good socks

CAUSE WHEN IT'S ALL SAID, IT STILL ISN'T DONE

It will unfold before you **this** season, **this** day

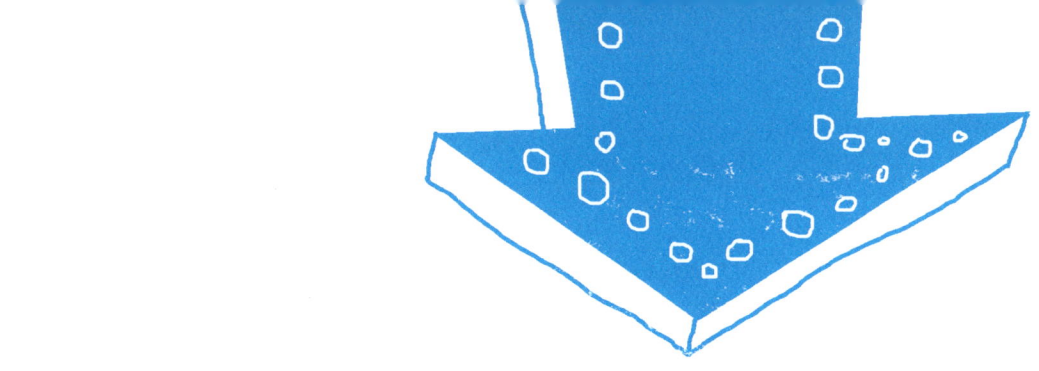

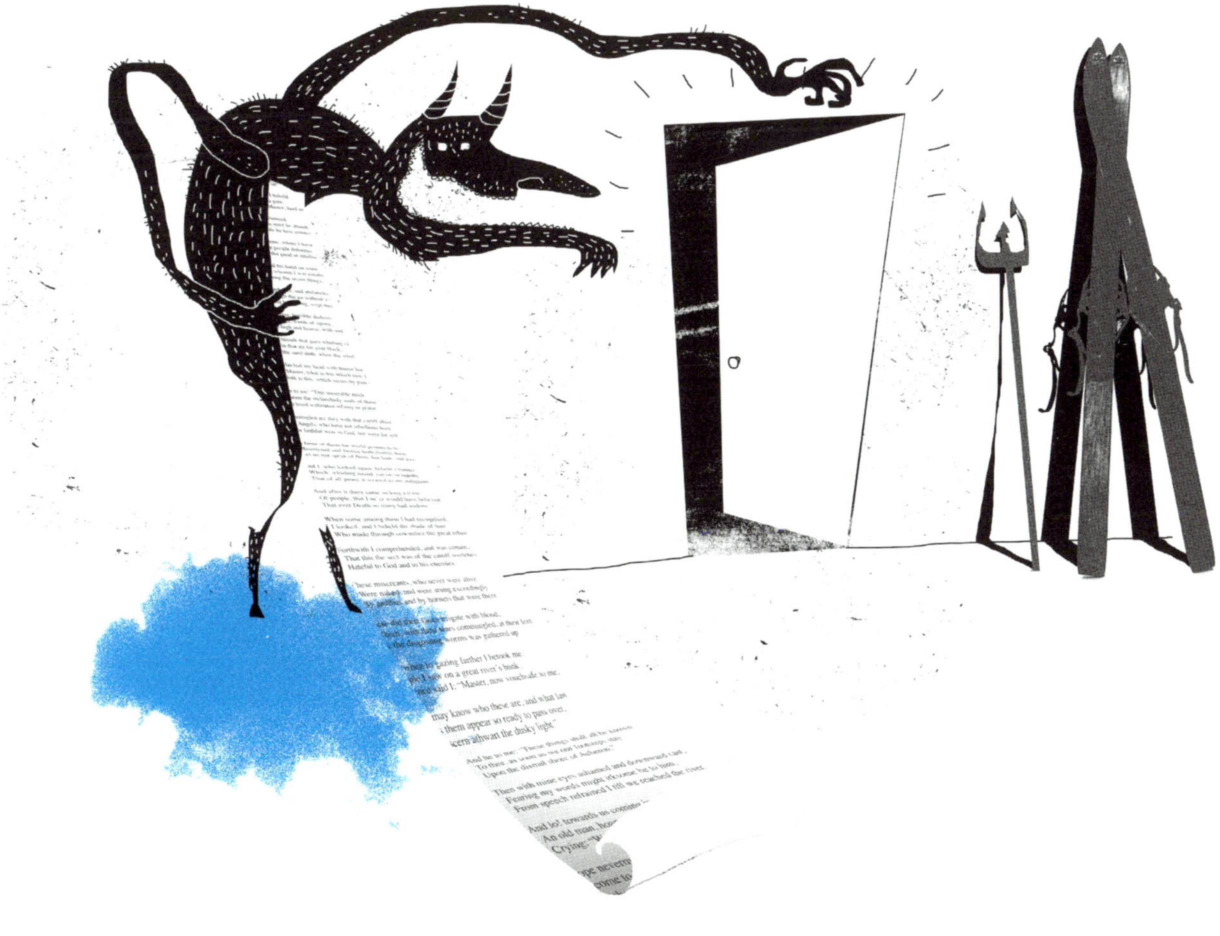
When some among them I had recognised,
I looked, and I beheld the shade of him
Who made through cowardice the great refusal.
Forthwith I comprehended, and was certain,
That this the sect was of the caitiff wretches
Hateful to God and to his enemies.
These miscreants, who never were alive,
Were naked, and were stung exceedingly
By gadflies and by hornets that were there.
worms was gathered up
farther I betook me,
on a great river's bank
"Master, now vouchsafe to me,
may know who these are, and what law
them appear so ready to pass over,
athwart the dusky light."
Then with mine eyes ashamed and downward cast,
Fearing my words might irksome be to him,
From speech refrained I till we reached the river.
And lo! towards us coming
An old man,
Crying: